Copyright

Indoor Gardening 101: C⌟arden in the Comfort of Your Home

March 2014

Pauline Waldeck

Copyright © 2014

All rights reserved.

Contents

About the Author

Pauline Waldeck is a passionate author and small business owner, residing in the vibrant city of Melbourne, Australia she owns several small nurseries and also commits a large portion of her free time to organizing, planning and consulting regarding community gardens.

The Gardening 101 Series

Be sure to check out the entire series! All books written by Pauline Waldeck are available on Amazon.com and Amazon.co.uk

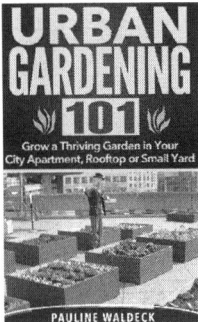

Introduction

I want to thank you and congratulate you for downloading the book, Indoor Gardening 101: Grow a Gorgeous Garden in the Comfort of Your Home

This book contains a comprehensive guide on how to plant, grow and maintain your very own container indoor garden at home. Indoor gardening is far more than just putting plants in pots. A well planned and set out indoor garden is a work of art, and gardening in itself is a fantastic hobby to take up.

After reading this book, you will realize just how fun and rewarding container gardening can be.

After reading this book you will be equipped with a vast knowledge of container indoor gardening, you will be aware of the benefits of indoor gardening, the required tools, how to correctly plant and select plants for your indoor garden along with tips for maintaining your plants, soil and preventing any pests.

Thanks again for downloading this book, I hope you enjoy it!

Bonus Content

As a token of my appreciation I would like to give you access to my exclusive bonus content.

You're only a click away from receiving:

Exclusive pre-release access to my latest gardening eBooks

Free eBooks during promotional periods

Simply navigate to http://shredded-society.com/Gardening101.html to receive this bonus content.

As this is a limited time offer it would be a shame to miss out, I recommend grabbing these bonuses at your earliest convenience.

What is Indoor Gardening

Indoor gardening can be defined as creating a garden environment in a limited space. This type of gardening is particularly beneficial for people living in apartments without enough space. Indoor gardening is also a great solution for people who want to have fresh produce during the winter.

Indoor gardening can also be incorporated as part of the heating or air conditioning system of your homes. Indoor gardening prolongs the natural life span of the flowers during the winter.

You can choose to buy young or grown plants and transfer them into pots. You can also start experimenting on different varieties and types of plants available. However, some less popular or newer variety plants are not yet sold in stores so you may also try to grow your own seeds. Seeds tend to be cheaper than grown plants but they do require more attention and time.

Benefits of Indoor Gardening

Indoor gardening is one of the best ways to incorporate natural and greener lifestyle in the comfort of your own home.

Controlled temperature

You have control over the temperature and environment of your indoor garden. Some plants like herbs are particularly fragile if they are planted outdoors. They can easily be ruined by rain, wind and direct sunlight. Indoor gardening methods can keep your plants safe from environmental factors.

Eliminates parasites

Parasites are less likely to attack your plants if they are planted indoors. You will still need to monitor the condition of plants since parasites can still find their way inside but the amount of parasite will most likely be fewer than if they are planted outside.

Versatile location

Indoor gardening gives more option for people who live in apartments and condominiums. Indoor gardening systems can adapt to suit the space available. Even people living in apartment spaces can now have fresh produce and enjoy seeing fresh flowers. You can choose to grow plants in window boxes or have your pot of herbs in the kitchen.

Economical

Indoor gardening tends to more productive and less expensive that traditional gardening. Once you have established a good indoor gardening system, you do not have to spend much on fertilizers and pest control. Most indoor plants also require less water. The risk of disease is greatly reduced so you will have more produce with less money and time.

Healthier environment

People living in the city are exposed to high levels of pollution, toxins and synthetic chemicals. Growing an indoor garden can clean about 87% of toxins in the air in 24 hours. They also produce oxygen which contributes to a healthier environment. Plants also increase your well being and are even proven to calm anxiety.

Things required for your Indoor Garden

Even if you have enough outdoor space, growing your own indoor garden can keep your house more lively and beautiful. Here are some of the supplies that you will need in staring your garden.

Choosing containers

Window boxes are one of the most popular herb containers since they are tailored to fill windows. However, you can also use pots and square boxes. The deeper the pot, the healthier the herb will be. Containers without drainage can be filled with an inch of gravel to serve as a water reservoir.

You can use pots and other used containers but make sure that you properly clean them in bleach and water. Also ensure that it has proper drainage holes so that excess water can be removed from the pot.

You can also choose to use seed starting kits since they already contain the necessary materials for growing seedlings. Some gardeners plant the seeds in a shallow tray then transport the sprout into larger containers.

Growing medium

You need to have an appropriate growing medium to ensure beautiful plants and optimal harvest. Seedlings are usually very delicate. You have to place them in a sterile and fresh seedling soil that is fluffy and light to the touch. Remember that if the growing medium is not sterile or is too wet, the plant can easily be pestered with disease.

You can start to use bagged seed soil or choose compressed pellets that can expand when wet. Since the seed already contains the necessary nutrient for the plant's development, adding fertilizer is not necessary.

Indoor garden fertilizer

Remember that different plants have different fertilizer requirement. Also, indoor fertilizer is different from traditional gardening so purchase fertilizer that is specifically labelled for indoor gardening.

Trowel

Trowels are the main tool needed for indoor gardening. Try to choose trowels that are made of steel since they tend to be stronger. Trowels that come with handle and blade are often more durable than other types.

Watering can

A watering can is an essential gardening tool. It can be used for spot watering or to distribute fertilizers in your pots.

Transplanting spade

A transplanting spade has a long and narrow blade that can get into the small corners of your garden. Using a transplanting spade cab also reduce the damage to other plants. You can also use this to dig deeper holes.

Fork

A garden fork is used to safely lift the roots of your plants. It can also be used to separate overgrown roots or to harvest your produce. Choose steel bladed forks since they are stronger.

Utility bag

A utility bag is essential when you start to weed your garden. You will need a utility bag to place garden debris and weeds. Collapsible bags and lightweight baskets are popular options.

Pruners

Keep your garden pristine by trimming overgrown shrubs. The by-pass pruners are more effective in making cleaner cuts than anvil pruners. Pruners with a swivel handle are also easier on the wrist.

Designing your Indoor Garden

Creating a beautiful indoor garden can be more complicated that what most people think. Here are some tips and techniques in designing your own garden.

Garden preparation

There are typically two indoor gardening styles: the hydroponic and the container gardening. A hydroponic garden is a type of indoor gardening that uses fertilized water and soil for the plants. Hydroponic gardens are beneficial for people who want to produce a lot of plants in a limited space. This type of gardening is also more applicable for growing herbs and vegetables.

Container gardens are beneficial for people who like to rearrange their plants around the house. Container gardens offer more flexibility and variety. Container gardens are popular for people who want to grow various types of plants in different sizes.

Designing a hydroponic garden

Step 1: Choose a system

You can design your hydroponic garden in different ways but they tend to follow the same theme: the water tank is located at the bottom and shelves of plants are place on top. A pump system provides water for the plants and the excess is drained in the original tank.

Some gardeners place live fish in the tank. This will naturally fertilize the water and create an ideal mixture for the plants. You can also create your hydroponics system using recyclable materials such as plastic bottles. Try to use one large container rather than small ones. A large container is also more ideal in growing large quantity of the same produce.

Step 2: Choose the location

Most hydroponic gardens will thrive when they are exposed to sunlight. Choose a space near the window where it can get enough sunlight. You can also use shelving until or a used bookshelf for your gardening system.

Step 3: Set up your system

A commercial hydroponics system usually comes with specific instructions and you will need to follow the direction when setting up your garden. If you are making your own system, start by placing the tank at the bottom of the shelves. Place the plant containers near the tank then attach the water pump to the shelves.

Designing a container garden

Step 1: Choose the containers

You have a wide variety of containers to choose from. You can choose traditional pots or use old vases as well as recycled plastic bottles. Look for containers with holes at the bottom for drainage.

Step 2: Creating a potting mix

You can either purchase or create your own potting mix. Making your own mix will guarantee the quality of the soil and will help you save money. You need one part coir peat, two parts compost and one part vermiculite. Soak the coir peat to rehydrate it. Mix the peat and vermiculite then add the compost.

Step 3: Set up your garden

You will need to create a shelving system if you plan to grow a large indoor garden. Otherwise, designing your container garden is a matter of preference. You can have fun deciding where to put them and which plants go together. Generally, medium sized flowering plants are placed on tables and counter tops. Shrubs and ferns can be placed beside large furniture.

Soil Preparation

Soil can make or break your garden, therefore it's crucial to pay attention to detail when preparing to soil so your plants will flourish.

Garden soil is too heavy and often contaminated with weed seeds, bugs and bacteria all of which we don't want.

Instead, use potting mix. Potting mix is very well aerated, sterile, lightweight, and contains a good balance of organic material and mineral particles such as peat, sand, and perlite.

Purchase a packaged, sterilized, soilless potting mix at your local garden center or nursery. If you require a large quantity, the majority of nurseries sell potting mix in bulk. I'd recommend trying different brands in order to see which ones are easiest to wet and which ones have the best moisture holding capacity and drainage properties. That said, don't over which brand of potting mix you purchase; caring for your plants properly after you plant them is far more important than choosing the perfect potting soil anyway.

If you're planning on growing plants in large containers, you'll be quite surprised at how much potting soil you need to fill each container. However it's worth noting that you do not have to fill each whole container with potting mix. Most roots will penetrate 10 to 12 inches into the soil. Using anu more than that and you're essentially just wasting soil.

My strategy I generally use in order to use less soil is to place empty plastic coke and milk bottles in the bottom portion of the container, and then throw the potting mix on top. Voila! Your container will now be lighter and much easier to move, you'll be recycling to help the environment, and you won't have to buy as much potting mix.

Continuously planting in the same soil from previous years is generally bad news for your plants. Over time the soil nutrition begins to deplete, and the soil likely has diseases, fungal spores, and insects within it.

A few tips to salvage your old potting mix are as follows:

Start fresh by replacing the old potting mix in each year. Repurpose the old mix by throwing it into other parts of your garden.

Use the old soil in the bottom third of your pots as opposed to using the plastic container strategy, place your new soil on top of the old soil.

Empty out your containers or pots and give them a good clean, while doing so you can amend the old potting mix with some new potting mix, refilling the pots.

Selecting plants for your Indoor Garden

People can benefit greatly from indoor gardens. Here are some of the best plants for your homes.

Houseplants for fresh air

Studies show that houseplants can help filter the air around them. Here are some of the best indoor houseplants that can improve air quality.

Aloe Vera

This is a sun loving plant that is easy to grow. Aloe Vera helps clear benzene and formaldehyde which typically comes from chemical based cleaners and paint. It can be placed in a kitchen window that is exposed to more sunlight. Aloe Vera gel can also be used to heal cuts and bruises acquired from cooking.

Spider plant

The spider plant is one of the most resilient houseplants. It has a lot of leaves and small white flowers. This is perfect for people who tend to forget about watering their plants. Spider plant also helps filter formaldehyde, carbon monoxide and xylene.

Gerber daisy

This daisy is a brightly colored plant that is effective in removing trichloroethylene from the air. It is also good at filtering benzene which is emitted from paint and ink. You can place it in your laundry room but make sure to give it a lot of sunlight.

Snake plant

The snake plant is also known as the mother-in-law's tongue. This can filter out formaldehyde which tends to come from cleaning products and personal care products. This plant do not like too much light and thrives in humid conditions.

Golden pothos

This is a fast growing plant that tends to cascade from its pot. It is highly recommended that you plant this in a hanging basket. You can place it in your garage to help filter out car exhaust. This plant also tends to stay green in color even if it is kept indoors.

Chrysanthemum

Chrysanthemum is a colorful flower that can brighten any room. It also filters out benzene which is commonly emitted from glue, plant and plastic. Chrysanthemum likes bright light so you need to place it in an open window.

Red-edged dracaena

The red color of the leaves can bring an instant pop of color in your room. This plant can grow tall enough to reach your ceiling. This plant can filter xylene and trichloroethylene which is emitted from indoor lacquers and varnish.

Weeping fig

The weeping fig is a ficus plant that can filter air pollutants that is brought by carpeting and furniture. Taking care of the weeping fig can be complicated but once you have the watering and lighting conditions right, the plant will surely last a long time.

Azalea

Azalea is a beautiful flowering shrub that can filter out formaldehyde from wood and foam insulation. Azaleas tend to survive better in cool environment. They can greatly improve your basement air if you find a good spot for it.

Warneck dracaena

The warneck dracaena can combat air pollutants from oil and varnish. This plant tends to grow easily even without direct sunlight. This is a very striking ornamental plant especially if it grows beyond 12 feet.

Chinese evergreen

The Chinese evergreen is an easy plant to take care of. It can also filter toxin in the air. It tends to produce beautiful red berries even if it is not exposed to direct sunlight.

Bamboo palm

The bamboo plant is also known as reed palm which tends to filter out benzene and trichloroethylene. This plant is also ideal to place around furniture since it can absorb formaldehyde gas.

Houseplants for beginners

Beginners at indoor gardening can first experiment with plants and flowers that are easy to take care of.

Island Pine

The Island Pine is one of the best trees to decorate in Christmas or as a holiday gift. It instantly gives a cozy feeling into any room. The secret in taking care of this pine is to give it ample light. Placing it in low light can make it turn brown.

Placing it in a dry place can make it susceptible to spider mites.

Peperomia

Peperomia adds colorful, waxy foliage and adds diversity in any room without taking too much space. Keep this plant in low to medium light and allow the soil surface to dry before watering.

Dracaena

Dracaena is a beautiful houseplant that resembles a corn without the ears. You can plant several stems together to achieve a fuller appearance. Cut the cane one or two feet above the soil if it grows too tall. This plant needs medium to bright light.

Zeezee plant

This plant is also being referred to as the eternity plant since it can last for a very long time. It is a succulent plant that can live in low light. Its leaves are so durable that it is sometimes mistaken as plastic. It is also slow growing so you do not have to trim often.

Hoya

Hoya or also known as the wax plant has green leaves and pink flowers. You can allow the plant to climb or just let it trail in a hanging basket. Its flowers are especially fragrant and it also does not need too much water.

Rubber tree

The rubber tree is an old fashioned tree that gets its name from its sticky sap. Its big and dark green leaves are very beautiful and can serve as a dramatic accent to your room.

Cast-iron plant

The cast iron plant can withstand neglect, low light and a wide range of temperatures. It tends to grow slowly so you have to purchase a plant that is near to the size you want. This plant is nearly indestructible.

Jade plant

The jade plant can survive for many years without too much water as long as it is exposed in bright light. It looks good combined with other cacti. It grows best if it is left in a cool room and just water it enough to prevent its leaves from shrivelling.

African violet

African violet is a slow growing plant that is characterized by its dark leaves and colorful flowers. This plant thrives in direct sunlight but not in hot temperatures. They tend to bloom better when they are placed under fluorescent light rather than a window.

Amaryllis

This is a house plant that blooms from a huge bulb and it produces a thick flower stalk. It can produce about six trumpet shaped flowers. Cool temperatures can prolong its flowers. Stop watering the plant once the flower blooms to force dormancy. Start watering again after a two month period.

Christmas kalanchoe

This plant need long fall nights to encourage bud growth. It has green, glossy and succulent leaves that are topped with red, pink pr even yellow flower. The flower of this plant can last for many months.

This is not a difficult plant to maintain but getting them to bloom once again can be challenging. Subject them to a 14 hour night for two months to encourage flower bud growth.

Indoor herb and spice garden

Herbs and spices can be expensive when bought at the market. They are also less flavourful if they are not fresh. Fortunately, you can easily grow your own herbs and spices in large pots and keep them in your kitchen. You only need few items to start your own indoor herb garden.

When choosing which herb or spice to plant in a window box, choose plants that have similar needs. Most indoor herbs and spices are faster to grow if it has been transplanted. Here are some of the best herbs for indoor gardening.

Lemongrass

Lemongrass is one of the easiest herbs to grow. Purchase a stalk from the market and look for one that has plenty of stem. Make sure that the base is intact. Trim it and place in water. The stalk will produce new shoots.

Chives

Chives do not require too much sunlight and they are also fast growing. Pull chives from an established plant and place it in a pot with soil. Cover with more potting soil then cut about one third off the top to stimulate growth.

Mint

Spearmint and peppermint grow like weeds. These herbs are invasive and hearty which means that they can overpower other herbs. Try to plant them in a separate container. Remember that peppermint has more flavor than spearmint so if you lack space, peppermint is a better choice.

Start growing your peppermint with seeds and not with leaf cuttings. Plant in a potting soil and try to keep it in the shade.

Parsley

Parsley is one of the easiest herbs to grow but its seeds can be difficult to germinate. However, it does not require too much maintenance once it starts to grow. Remember that thus herb tends to grow slower so try to plant more of this herb.

Oregano

The Greek variety of oregano is easiest to grow but it needs at least 6 hours of sun exposure in a day.

Thyme

Thyme also needs a lot of sunlight and may even need supplement sunlight. One of the popular herbs is the lemon thyme which can be used like regular thyme and has a citrus like flavor.

Rosemary

Remember that rosemary likes to remain dry and it does not necessarily need a rich soil. There are many varieties of rosemary available so choose one that can fit your space. Rosemary herbs that remain compact are better for indoor gardening.

Basil

Basil is an essential herb for cooking but it tends to be one of the most difficult herbs to grow. The best variety for indoor gardening is the African Blue and Spicy Globe.

Maintaining your Indoor Garden

Here are some tips and techniques on how you can keep your indoor garden looking good and staying healthy.

Sunshine

Most plants come with instructions about proper lighting. Here are some of them:

Direct light tag mean that the plant needs about at least six hours of sunlight a day. It should also be directly exposed to the sun.

Moderate light tag means that the plant needs direct sunlight for about four hours a day.

Indirect light means that the plant should be placed few feet away from direct sunlight. These types of plants do not need too much sunlight.

Low light tag plants can survive with ambient light and no direct sunlight. It is best placed in a room that does not get too much sun.

Remember that north facing windows do not receive too much light. Windows at the south are sunny most of the time while west and east windows receive sunlight at a certain time of the day. Get to know which part of your house gets sunlight to know where you can place certain plants.

Water

There is no solid rule on how often you should water your plants. Heat and sunlight can dry the soil at varying rates. Remember to check your soil from time to time.

"Water steadily or evenly" This means that you have to water your plant whenever the soil feels dry.

"Water moderately" This means that you can allow at least an inch of soil to dry before watering.

Water your plants by saturating them thoroughly until water is drained through the bottom of the pot. Throw the water that is collected in the saucer if it is not reabsorbed within a day.

Refill your watering can and set it at room temperature. This will ensure that the additives like fluoride are dissipated from the water. Keep plants that need constant attention in plain sight so that you cannot forget about them.

Plants and containers

Always be careful in purchasing plants. Look for plants with firm and healthy stems. Stay away from plants that have more stems than leaves. Remember that you should use a container that is about the same size or about two inches larger than the old pot of the plant.

Replanting plants in a very big pot means that it will need extra soil and water which can rot the roots. Also, ensure that your plant pot always have a drainage hole at the bottom.

Terra cotta pots are more durable but you can also consider fibreglass and resin. These materials tend to hold moisture longer which means that you do not have to water often. Use saucers that are glazed inside to catch any water from the pot.

How to repot plants

Remove your plants from their plastic pots. Make sure to water your plants thoroughly to strengthen the roots.

Hold the stem between your fingers and turn the pot upside down. Gently remove the plant from the pot. You can trim the roots to make it easier for you to remove the plants.

Place a stone at the drainage of the new pot to prevent the soil from draining. Put an inch of soil or potting mixture in the pot. Place the plant at the center.

Add soil around the plants. Use a stick to adjust the soil and to tamp around the roots. Do not fill the entire pot. Leave at least quarter inch space from the rim. This will help hold the water so that it would not spill over.

Pests & Diseases

Common Pests

The following are common pests and diseases you may run into while gardening, the key to a healthy garden is knowing how to identify and treat common pests and diseases, so take note to ensure you are able to identify these should they (unfortunately) find their way into your garden.

Aphids
Aphids are small white critters that congregate on stems and nodes, they suck the life out of plants. To eliminate Aphids a strong spray from your garden hose will dislodge them. Ladybugs can also rid Aphids.

Black vine weevils
during late spring and early summer, these weevils are harmless pupae resting in your gardens soil. The adults emerge and eat the foliage of dozens of perennials (and lay eggs for the next generation while they're at it). The typical sign is notched leaf edges, particularly lower down on the plant where the insects find more shelter. Starting in early fall, the newly hatched grubs eat roots. Counterattack in fall by

releasing beneficial nematodes (roundworms), available from most garden centers and mail-order sources; apply according to the labels instructions.

Leaf miners

leaf miners form a brown, tan or clear traceries, tunnels or channels on affected leaves but hardly ever kill the plant. I recommend removing and discarding the affected leaves, the plant will generate new ones.

Root nematodes

Plants affected with root nematodes develop severely distorted growth.

Remove the plants out and discard them before they spread.

Voles

Voles come out of their underground tunnels and chew on perennials, specifically the leaves but also roots, seeds, and bulbs. Voles are slightly larger than mice, with a shorter tail and smaller ears. The best deterrent for Voles is a cat.

Castor oil as a repellent also works quite well.

Common Diseases

Anthracnose
This fungi attacks beans, vine crops, tomatoes, and peppers.
Look out for small, discolored leaf spots or dead twigs.
Prune off affected plant parts. Fungicides containing copper
can help.

Club root
This fungus infects mainly cole crops. Symptoms include
stunted growth, wilting, poor development, and swollen
lumps on the roots.
Avoid planting susceptible crops in infected soil.

Corn smut
This fungus disease causes large, mutant-looking, white to
gray swellings on corn ears.
Prevent the disease by rotating crops.

Damping off
This fungus rots the stems of young plants near the soil line.
Prevent by planting only in pasteurized planting soil and
avoiding overwatering.

Fusarium wilt
The symptoms are yellowing leaves and stunted growth,
followed by wilting and plant death.
After plants are infected, no cure is possible.
Build your soil's health so that it contains lots of beneficial
microorganisms.

Leaf spots and blights

Several fungi show up first as circular spots on plant leaves. The spots increase in size until the leaves die and fall off. The fungi spread if overhead watering wets the foliage. Solve with botanical and biological fungicides first, using copper-based fungicides only as a last resort.

Mildew

These 2 fungi produce similar symptoms: a white, powdery coating on leaves. The fungi disfigure plants but may not kill them. Use potassium bicarbonate, superfine horticultural oil, or neem oil to treat infected plants.

Root rot

Several fungal root diseases cause susceptible plants to turn yellow, wilt, and die. Plants are susceptible when the soil is too moist or poorly aerated. The fungi can survive in the soil for many years. Prevent root rot by building healthy, well-drained soil.

Rust fungus

Rust fungus is most prevalent in humid and damp conditions. Provide good air circulation, remove and destroy infected foliage, and keep your tools clean.

Verticillium wilt

This fungus affects tomatoes, eggplant, potatoes, raspberries, strawberries, roses, Japanese maples, olives, and cherries. Look for wilting and yellow leaves. The leaves may curl up before falling off. Choose resistant varieties, and practice crop rotation.

Viruses

This group of incurable diseases infects vegetables, brambles, strawberries, trees, and flowering plants. The leaves develop mottled yellow, white, or light green patches. Flowers may develop off-color patches, and fruit ripens unevenly. Aphids, leafhoppers, nematodes, and whiteflies spread the virus as they move from plant to plant.

Prevention is the only strategy.

Overcoming Common Indoor Gardening Problems

Starting an indoor garden has its own set of problems but fortunately none of these are insurmountable. The benefits derived from growing an indoor garden also outweigh its disadvantage. Once you identify the common problems in indoor gardening, you can devise plans on how to avoid it and grow a beautiful garden.

Not enough light

Plants need sunlight to grow. It can be difficult to grow a lot of plants if you live in a place that does not get too much sunlight. Houseplants can live under indoor lights but vegetables and herbs will need more than that. You can solve this problem by placing it directly under sunlight or installing artificial light system.

Bacteria and infections

Indoor gardens can also be susceptible to disease and infections. The best way to solve this problem is to spot it right away.

As soon as you spot the insects, rinse their leaves with warm water then with mild soapy water. If you spot eggs, webs of cocoons, remove it with a cotton swab.

Keep new plants away from your houseplants for a few weeks to avoid spreading pests. Take this time to inspect your new plant for bugs and insects.

Neglect your plants a little bit. Allow them to dry a little and limit the amount of fertilizer that you give. This discourages insects and fungus.

Watch and look for pests each time you water your plants.

Disease can easily be spread on debris so pick fallen leaves and remove any dead plant. Also, keep the space under the container clean.

Disinfect any pruning tools that you use in a water and bleach solution.

Humidity problems

Certain plants require moisture to survive. Appliances such as heater can dry out the air around your house. The best way to avoid this is by spraying the leaves with water at least once a day. A humidifier can also prevent the air from drying out.

Overuse of fertilizer

Too much fertilizer can also be bad on plants. One sign that you are using fertilizer is if the leaves are turning brown. Ask the shop where you bought the plant for some tips and advice on how much fertilizer you should give.

Improper watering

You can drown the plants by giving too much water and you can dry them by giving them little water. If the leaves are decaying, you are probably giving them too much water. Make sure that the containers have holes for proper drainage.

Conclusion

Thank you again for downloading this book!

I hope this book was able to help you kick-start your indoor garden.
You've now been equipped with all the necessary knowledge to select the right plants and tools to grow yourself a fantastic indoor garden that will brighten up your home, as mentioned in the book indoor gardening has a huge variety of benefits and the feeling of accomplishment felt from growing a successful, vibrant indoor garden are endless.

Now, it's time to go out there and get to work on your garden.

Finally, if you enjoyed this book, please take the time to share your thoughts and post a review on Amazon. It'd be greatly appreciated!

Thank you and happy gardening!

8870098R00023

Printed in Great Britain
by Amazon.co.uk, Ltd.,
Marston Gate.